Lindsey Vonn

The Fastest Woman on

Skis for Kids

Daisy Sparkle

Copyright

Table of Contents

Introduction

She was born in a place that is very different from the tall mountains and Olympic hills where she would one day make history. A state known for its cold winters but not for snowboarding is where she was born. Some of the best skiers in the world grew up in places like the Swiss Alps or the Colorado Rockies. Lindsey, on the other hand, didn't grow up in a place with steep slopes like most skiers do. There was no stopping her from having big dreams, though.

Lindsey learned to ski for the first time when she was only two years old. Alan, her father, used to compete in ski races when he was younger, and he taught Lindsey how much he loved the sport. Lindsey was hooked as soon as she slid down her first snowy hill. She loved how the cold air rushed past her face and how exciting it was to go faster and faster down the hill.

But Minnesota wasn't exactly a great place to ski. The hills were not very big, and there weren't many chances to practice. To find places for Lindsey to train, she and her family would go to nearby states or vacations. As a child, she didn't mind putting in extra work because it made her love for the sport grow. She loved it. Lindsey loved skiing so much that it wasn't just a sport for her. She felt like she was flying every time she put her boots on her skis.

Her family played a big role in her early success. Their support meant that she could follow her dreams, even if it meant long trips to the ski hill and a lot of practice. Her father was her coach and biggest fan. He pushed her to do her best and taught her how important it is to work hard and not give up. He knew from personal experience that it took more than natural skill to be a great skier. It took hard work, focus, and a lot of heart. That's all Lindsey had.

The family of Lindsey knew when she was 10 years old that she needed to learn with the best if she wanted to follow her dream of becoming a professional skier. Moving to Vail, Colorado, was a big choice for them. Lindsey could train on real slopes and compete with other young skiers who shared her dream. This was the start of a great journey for Lindsey. Her new ski runs were some of the toughest in the country, and she loved every second of it.

Lindsey had a big heart for a young girl. She worked out every day, even when it was cold or she was tired. Her dream was getting closer with each run down the mountain, so she didn't mind how hard it was. She had a clear goal: to represent the United States in the Winter Olympics and win gold.

Lindsey's first Olympic Games were in Salt Lake City in 2002, when she was only 16 years old. That year, she didn't win a gold, but she did gain something even more valuable: experience. It took time for great things to happen, and Lindsey knew that. She had to push herself even more, work even harder, and be ready for anything that came her way. The world might not know her name yet, but Lindsey was set on making sure that everyone would one day.

But Lindsey's path wasn't always easy. There were times when she got hurt, had setbacks, and had problems that would have made many champions give up. Lindsay, not so much. She got back up every time she fell. Each hurt was just another problem to solve. Lindsey thought that ending her efforts was the only way to fail, which she was never going to do.

It wasn't just Lindsey Vonn's speed or amazing skill on the hills that made her stand out; it was her unwavering drive and refusal to give up. People looked up to her not only because she won races, but also because she showed them how to be strong. She was brave, worked hard, and believed that you can always find a way to keep going, no matter how bad things get.

Everyone didn't know that the Minnesota girl who used to ski down small hills would soon be one of the best snowboarders the world had ever seen. She broke records, won gold at the

Olympics, and encouraged her peers to follow

their goals, no matter where they came from.

Chapter 1:Growing Up in Minnesota

Lindsey Vonn's road to becoming a world-class skier began in a place that isn't known for its high mountains or high-end ski resorts. She was born in Saint Paul, Minnesota, on October 18, 1984. Minnesota is known for its lakes and snowy winters, but it's not usually what you think of when you think of skiing winners. Still, it was on these small, snowy hills in Minnesota that Lindsey first fell in love with snowboarding.

Even though Lindsey wasn't born into a family of skilled athletes, her dad, Alan, used to be a competitive skier when he was younger. He wanted to be the best skier in the world, but an accident stopped him. He still taught Lindsey how much he loved the sport. Lindsey started skiing with her family when she was only two years old. They taught her how to balance and glide down small hills. Skiing might have been a fun winter exercise for most kids, but Lindsey did it because it was her thing from the start. A short time later, everyone on the slopes could tell she wasn't like other kids.

The winters in Minnesota were long and hard, with lots of snow and very low temperatures. What Lindsey loved was it. No matter how cold it was, she would take her family to the nearby ski hills whenever she could. Buck Hill, a small ski area outside of Minneapolis, was her best place to practice. The mountain wasn't very big, but it didn't need to be. Every time Lindsey ran, she used the whole hill to work on her turns and improve her skills.

Lindsey was determined to get better even when she was young. She wasn't just skiing for fun; she was also very competitive. She loved going down the hill quickly and always tried to go faster. Even though Buck Hill wasn't the biggest or steepest hill, it was perfect for Lindsey because it gave her a place to practice and helped her love the sport.

She had a coach named Erich Sailer who saw her promise when she was a child and was one of the most important people in her early life. At Buck Hill, he taught a lot of young skiers, but he knew Lindsey was different. Along with his help, Lindsey improved all of her snowboarding skills, from perfecting her form to keeping her speed in check on rough terrain. Coach Sailer had faith in Lindsey, which made her feel better about herself. Lindsey wasn't just good at skiing; she wanted to be the best.

But Lindsey had to work hard to get the right chances because she grew up in Minnesota. There weren't as many big mountains in Minnesota as there were in other places, so Lindsey had to go somewhere else to compete at a high level. Her family was very encouraging, and they would often drive hours to take her to ski races in nearby states so she could compete with other very good young skiers. Lindsey's first taste of what it would be like to ski at a higher level was in these events, and she did great under the stress.

Lindsey's love for skiing only grew stronger as she got older. As early as age 10, she was already running in important races, often against girls much older than her. She not only competed, she won. Lindsey did well on the small hills in Minnesota, which showed she was ready for bigger problems.

Her family did something that changed their lives to help her reach her goals. She could train on real mountains and ski with some of the best young athletes in the country when they moved to Vail, Colorado. It was hard for Lindsey to leave Minnesota, but she had to keep improving as a racer. Lindsey had to leave her friends, the place where she fell in love with snowboarding for the first time, and the things she was used to. But she knew in her heart that it was the right thing to do.

The things Lindsey learned in Minnesota will always be with her, even though she moved away. Being outside in the cold and snow had made her tough, and the small hills had taught her how to make the most of every chance.

Minnesota was the start of her trip, and it will always be a part of her story.

Being raised in Minnesota gave Lindsey more than just a love of skiing. It also gave her the drive, discipline, and toughness she would need to become the best skier in the world.

Chapter 2:Early Competitions:

Lindsey's First Races

It wasn't enough for Lindsey Vonn to just ski for fun; she was also a racer, even when she was a little girl. The first ski races Lindsey did were as soon as she could. She loved more than just going fast down the hill. She loved competing with other people, seeing how fast she could go, and always trying to go faster. Their first races were not very big, but they were the beginning of something much bigger.

Lindsey raced at Buck Hill in Minnesota, which is also where she trained at the nearby ski area. Lindsey thought it was the best place to learn, even though it wasn't a huge mountain like those in Colorado or Switzerland. Every time she ran, she worked hard to improve her speed and practice her turns. Lindsey already knew what she wanted when she was seven or eight years old: she wanted to win.

One of her first races was in her town, and the other kids were a lot older than she was. Lindsey wasn't the biggest or strongest person, but she was fearless, which made her stand out. Other

kids were scared, but Lindsey was focused.
When it was her turn to race, she flew down the
hill so fast and so accurately that everyone who
saw her knew she was something special. She
didn't just ski down the hill; she went up and
down it. She won the race by the time she got to
the finish line. There was no doubt that she was
strong, even though she was young.

Lindsey didn't just win by chance. She worked
out hard by skiing before and after school a lot
to get better at her turns and find her way around
the track. Lindsey got better with each race, and
soon, people in the local snowboarding

community knew her name. Coaches and other skiers started to notice the tough girl who could go faster and do better on turns than most kids her age.

Lindsey faced tougher hurdles as she competed in more events. The races got tougher, the hills got higher, and the competition got tougher. What Lindsey loved was it. She did well under stress, and the tougher the task, the more focused she became. She didn't mind losing; in fact, she believed that every race, win or lose, was a chance to get better.

She had one of her first big wins when she was only nine years old. At a regional competition, she skied against some of the best young skiers from Minnesota and states close by. The course was icy and hard because it was cold and wet. A lot of the racers had trouble, but Lindsey went at the course with ease. She skied quickly down the hill, and her skis didn't even notice the ice. When she got to the finish line, she was miles ahead of everyone else. She won first place.

Her family knew after that that she had something really special. They started going even farther for her runs, taking Lindsey to

Wisconsin and Michigan to compete in bigger events. These were Lindsey's first steps toward becoming the best. Each race was important, even though they were small compared to what she would face later. In addition to winning, she wanted to learn, grow, and push herself to be better.

As Lindsey moved up to tougher events, she had to deal with new problems. The races got tougher and longer, and the racers got older and more experienced. Lindsey wasn't scared, though. Instead, it made her stronger will. She learned something from every race, even the ones she didn't win. What went wrong? What could she do better? Lindsey wasn't just thinking about being the best right now; she was also thinking about how to be the best *in the future*.

A lot of what helped Lindsey do well in these early races was her guide, Erich Sailer. From the beginning, he saw Lindsey's promise and pushed her to keep getting better. He taught her how to deal with stress, stay calm at the starting line, and keep her eye on the finish line at all times. Lindsey learned a lot from him about how to deal with tough situations, like icy slopes, blinding snow, and the stress of big tournaments.

In races all over the country, Lindsey was often up against bigger, stronger skiers by the time she was a teenager. She never gave up, though. Each race brought her one step closer to her dream of playing in the Olympics. She had faith in herself.

These early races helped Lindsey become the winner she would become. That's how they taught her to get through tough races, deal with sadness, and never give up. More than anything else, they told her that the most important thing is to learn something new every time you ski

down the mountain, not to win every race.

Skiing Records Being Broken

People all over the world knew Lindsey Vonn's

name because she was so fast on the slopes and

always pushed the edges of what was possible in

skiing. She broke records, changed what it meant

to be a champion, and motivated millions of

people with her unwavering drive. She was one

of the best skiers of all time because she loved

the sport and wouldn't give up, even when she got hurt or had problems.

Along the way, Lindsey set her sights on one of the most prestigious goals in skiing: becoming the overall World Cup winner. For skiers, the World Cup is like a tough test. There is more than one race going on all over the world. To win the World Cup as a whole, you have to be the best in all four types of races: downhill, super-G, slalom, and giant slalom. It's a big deal to win this title once, but Lindsey didn't just want to win once; she wanted to conquer.

Lindsey made history when she won her first World Cup title as a whole in 2008. The downhill races, which are the fastest and riskiest in snowboarding, were her specialty. In downhill, skiers run down the mountain at very high speeds—often 80 miles per hour—while making sharp turns and huge jumps. Lindsey did very well in this high-pressure setting and was the fastest skier going down the hills. That season's win made her one of the best snowboarders in the world.

Lindsey wasn't done yet, though. Then she won the World Cup again in 2009, 2010, and 2012.

She was the first American woman to win the title four times. She was one of the most versatile skiers in history because she could compete at such a high level in so many sports. Lindsey always gave it her all, no matter what the race or course was, and most of the time, she won.

For Lindsey, one of the most important things in her career was to win gold at the Winter Olympics. In 2010, she did just that in Vancouver, Canada. The best skiers in the world were in the downhill event that Lindsey was in. There was a lot of stress, but Lindsey was ready.

She had spent her whole life getting ready for this moment. She skied with perfect form as she flew down the mountain, making every turn just right and going through the course at lightning speed. She looked up at the scoreboard when she crossed the finish line and saw that her time was the best! She was the first American woman to win an Olympic gold medal in the downhill, which made history.

There were more records Lindsey would break, though. During her career, she won 82 World Cup races, more than any other woman in history. People knew her as a brave skier who always pushed herself to go faster and take more risks. She was the best at everything, from downhill races where she blew past her opponents to super-G events where she made perfect turns.

The record-breaking success Lindsey had wasn't easy to get. She got hurt badly along the way, which would have ended anyone else's career. She broke bones, tore ligaments in her knee, and even got a concussion. But Lindsey always fought her way back after getting hurt. She worked hard for months in physical rehab to get stronger and get back on the slopes. When athletes had so many failures, some might have given up, but Lindsey wouldn't let her injuries define her. She always wanted to break records and win more titles, and she thought that each comeback made her stronger.

Lindsey participated in her last Winter Olympics in Pyeongchang, South Korea, in 2018. She was one of the oldest skiers in the race at 33 years old, but she still had the heart of a winner. She won third place in the downhill and became the oldest woman to ever win an Olympic alpine skiing gold. Over twenty years, she had an amazing career. Even in her last races, she continued to break barriers and set new marks.

As Lindsey got ready to stop competing in snowboarding, she left a legacy that would motivate athletes for years to come. With 82 World Cup wins and three Olympic medals, she is without a doubt one of the best skiers of all time. I will never forget her story because of how brave she was, how hard she worked, and how much she loved the sport.

Lindsey Vonn proved that having the heart to break records is just as important as having the skills. She showed that if you work hard and are determined, you can always reach your goals, no matter how hard things get.

Chapter 3:Life Beyond Skiing:

Hobbies and Interests

Even though Lindsey Vonn is known for her incredible skiing career, there's so much more to her life beyond the slopes. After dedicating most of her life to skiing, Lindsey has found new hobbies and interests that keep her busy, creative, and passionate.

Fitness has always been an important part of Lindsey's life, and even after retiring, she remains dedicated to staying active. She enjoys strength training, yoga, and running, and often shares her workouts with fans to inspire them to lead healthy, active lives. Her commitment to fitness led her to write a book called "Strong is the New Beautiful," where she talks about the importance of health, strength, and feeling confident inside and out. Through her work, she encourages people to take care of their bodies and embrace their inner strength.

Another big part of Lindsey's life is her love for animals, especially dogs. Lindsey has a special bond with her pets, and her dog Lucy, a King Charles Spaniel, is often by her side. She has a soft spot for animals in need and has rescued several dogs over the years. Lindsey frequently talks about how much joy her pets bring to her life, and she uses her platform to encourage people to adopt animals from shelters and rescue organizations. Her passion for animal welfare is just another way she gives back.

In addition to her love for animals, Lindsey is also committed to helping others through her charity work. In 2015, she created the Lindsey Vonn Foundation, which is dedicated to empowering young girls. The foundation provides scholarships, programs, and mentorship opportunities to help girls achieve their dreams, whether it's in sports, academics, or other areas. Lindsey wants to be a role model for young athletes and show them that with hard work, they can accomplish anything.

Lindsey also has a love for fashion and design. Since retiring from skiing, she's had more time to explore her creative side. She's worked with fashion brands and appeared on red carpets, always showcasing her style. Lindsey enjoys this new chapter in her life, where she can focus on different forms of self-expression.

Travel is another big part of Lindsey's life. During her skiing career, she traveled the world for competitions, but now she can travel purely for fun and adventure. She loves exploring new places, whether it's relaxing on a beach, hiking in the mountains, or visiting cities around the globe. Her curiosity about the world keeps her connected to new cultures and experiences.

Lindsey Vonn may have retired from professional skiing, but her life is still full of excitement, passion, and purpose. Whether she's staying active, spending time with her dogs, helping young athletes, or traveling the world,

Lindsey continues to inspire people to pursue their dreams and live life to the fullest. She shows that even after reaching the top of her sport, there's always room to grow, learn, and make a difference.

Fun Facts About Lindsey Vonn

1. She started skiing at just two years old!* Lindsey was practically born on skis. She first hit the slopes when she was only two years old, and from that moment, she was hooked. Her

love for skiing grew quickly, and she never looked back.

2. She holds the record for the most World Cup wins by a female skier.

Lindsey won 82 World Cup races during her career, the most by any female skier in history. She became famous for her incredible speed, power, and fearless attitude on the slopes.

3. Lindsey won an Olympic gold medal.

In the 2010 Winter Olympics in Vancouver, Lindsey won the gold medal in the downhill event. This made her the first American woman to win an Olympic gold in downhill skiing!

4. She loves animals, especially dogs.

Lindsey has a special bond with her dogs, including her King Charles Spaniel named Lucy. She often posts about them on social media and loves spending time with her furry friends.

5. She is a best-selling author.

Lindsey wrote a book called "Strong is the New Beautiful," where she shares her fitness tips and talks about how to stay strong—both physically and mentally. Her goal is to inspire others to be confident and healthy.

6. She's a great cook.

Lindsey loves to cook and has a passion for making healthy, delicious meals. She often shares recipes with her fans, showing them how to eat well while staying fit.

7. She's a huge fan of snowboarding too!

Even though she's known for her skiing, Lindsey enjoys snowboarding in her free time. She likes to switch things up and try different ways of enjoying the snow.

8. She's been in movies and TV shows.

Lindsey has made guest appearances in movies
and TV shows, including cameos in *Law &
Order* and *Hollywood Game Night*. She even
voiced a character in an animated series called
Freezing!

9. She loves fashion.

Lindsey has a passion for fashion and has
worked with several brands. She often attends
fashion shows and red-carpet events, showing
off her unique style when she's not wearing ski
gear.

10. She founded her charity.

Lindsey started the Lindsey Vonn Foundation in 2015, which helps young girls achieve their dreams through scholarships and mentorship programs. She's committed to giving back and inspiring others to reach their full potential.

Messages for Young Athletes

from Lindsey Vonn

1. Never give up, no matter what challenges you face.

Throughout her career, Lindsey faced many injuries and setbacks, but she never let those stop her. She came back stronger each time and always kept her eyes on her goals. Her message to young athletes is simple: *Don't quit when things get tough.* Whether you're injured, struggling with a skill, or feeling discouraged, keep pushing forward. Every challenge is an opportunity to learn and grow.

"In life and sports, you're going to face obstacles. It's how you handle them that defines you."

2. Believe in yourself.

Lindsey always believed in her abilities, even when others doubted her. When she was a young girl growing up in Minnesota, she didn't have huge mountains to train on, but she believed she could still become one of the best skiers in the world. Her message is that confidence in yourself and your dreams is key. *Believe that you can achieve great things, and never let anyone tell you otherwise.*

"You have to believe that you can be the best, even when the odds are stacked against you."

3. Hard work beats talent.

While Lindsey is naturally talented, she knows that talent alone isn't enough to succeed. She worked harder than anyone else to reach the top, practicing for hours every day, pushing herself in the gym, and staying focused on improving. Her advice for young athletes is that *hard work is the key to success.* No matter how gifted you are, dedication and practice will take you further than you ever thought possible.

"The only way to achieve your goals is to work hard every day and push yourself to be better."

4. It's okay to fail—learn from it.
Lindsey didn't win every race, and she experienced tough losses throughout her career. But instead of getting discouraged, she used failure as motivation to improve. Her message is that *failure is a part of life,* especially in sports. The important thing is to learn from it,

use it to get better and come back stronger the next time.

"Failing doesn't mean you're not good enough. It means you're brave enough to try again."

5. Take care of your body and mind.

Lindsey has always been committed to staying healthy, not just physically but mentally as well. She emphasizes the importance of taking care of your body through proper nutrition, rest, and exercise, but also making sure to take care of your mental health. *Being strong is about more than just muscles—it's about having a healthy mindset and being kind to yourself.*

"Your body and mind are your greatest tools—take care of them, and they'll take care of you."

6. Have fun and enjoy the process.

While Lindsey was fiercely competitive, she always remembered why she started skiing in the first place—because she loved it. Her message to young athletes is to *enjoy the sport you're playing.* Don't just focus on winning or losing; focus on having fun, making friends, and enjoying the journey. The memories you make along the way are just as important as the medals.

"At the end of the day, it's the joy of playing that matters most. Enjoy every moment and have fun!"

7. Support your teammates.

Lindsey always valued teamwork and encouraged her teammates, even in an individual sport like skiing. Her message is to *always be there for your teammates,* whether in practice or competition. Success is sweeter when shared, and being a good teammate means lifting others and celebrating their wins too.

"Being a champion isn't just about winning—it's about supporting the people around you and working together."

Q&A: Test Your Knowledge

1. At what age did Lindsey Vonn start skiing?

- A. 5

- B. 2

- C. 10

---

2. Which state did Lindsey grow up in before moving to Colorado to train?

- A. California

- B. Minnesota

- C. Utah

---

3. How many World Cup victories did Lindsey Vonn achieve in her career?

- A. 82

- B. 75

- C. 90

---

4. In which Winter Olympics did Lindsey Vonn win her first gold medal?

- A. 2014 Sochi

- B. 2010 Vancouver

- C. 2006 Turin

---

5. What type of dog does Lindsey Vonn have?

- A. King Charles Spaniel

- B. Golden Retriever

- C. Beagle

---

6. True or False: Lindsey Vonn also enjoys

snowboarding.

- A. True

- B. False

---

7. What is the title of Lindsey Vonn's book about fitness and confidence?

- A. *Strength and Speed*

- B. *Strong is the New Beautiful*

- C. *Ski to Success*

---

8. What is Lindsey Vonn's foundation focused on?

- A. Environmental conservation

- B. Supporting young girls and helping them achieve their dreams

- C. Building new ski resorts

---

9. In what year did Lindsey Vonn retire from competitive skiing?

- A. 2019

- B. 2017

- C. 2020

---

10. **True or False: Lindsey Vonn is the most successful female skier in World Cup history.**

- A. True

- B. False

Conclusion

Lindsey Vonn's journey from a young girl skiing on the small hills of Minnesota to becoming one of the greatest skiers of all time is an inspiring story of hard work, resilience, and determination. From the moment she first put on skis at just two years old, Lindsey showed a special passion for the sport, a passion that would carry her to the highest levels of skiing. But her story is about much more than just medals and records—it's about never giving up, believing in yourself, and using every challenge as an opportunity to grow.

As Lindsey climbed to the top of the skiing world, she faced countless obstacles, including serious injuries that threatened to end her career. Many athletes would have given up, but not Lindsey. She fought back from injury after injury, each time showing the world what it meant to have true grit and determination. Lindsey's ability to bounce back, even when things seemed impossible, is a powerful reminder to all of us that we can achieve great things if we're willing to keep going, no matter how hard it gets.

Throughout her career, Lindsey won 82 World Cup races, an Olympic gold medal, and numerous other titles, becoming the most successful female skier in history. She broke records that many thought were unbreakable and set new standards for what it meant to be an elite athlete. But what made Lindsey truly special wasn't just her ability to ski fast—it was her heart, her courage, and her love for the sport.

Lindsey's story doesn't end with her retirement from skiing. Off the slopes, she continues to make a difference in the world, whether through her charitable work with the Lindsey Vonn Foundation, her passion for promoting health and fitness, or her advocacy for animal rescue. She's shown that being a champion isn't just about winning races; it's about how you use your success to help others and inspire the next generation.

Through her foundation, Lindsey helps young girls achieve their dreams by providing scholarships and mentorship opportunities. She wants to give back and help others, just as she was helped by her family and coaches when she was a young skier. Lindsey's dedication to empowering young people shows that her legacy is about more than just sports—it's about making a positive impact on the world.

Lindsey's life beyond skiing is filled with exciting adventures, from traveling the world to pursuing her love for fashion, fitness, and animals. She continues to inspire millions of people with her strength, determination, and positive attitude. Whether she's training in the gym, hiking in the mountains, or spending time with her beloved dogs, Lindsey lives her life with the same drive and energy that made her a champion on the slopes.

Lindsey Vonn's story is a powerful example of what it means to follow your dreams, no matter where you start or what challenges you face. She reminds us that success isn't about how many times you win, but how many times you get back up after falling. Her journey teaches young athletes—and anyone with big dreams—that with hard work, perseverance, and belief in yourself, you can achieve incredible things.

As you think about Lindsey's story, remember that greatness isn't just for the fastest or the strongest—it's for those who are willing to put in the effort, push through difficulties, and keep going even when it's tough. Lindsey Vonn showed the world what it means to be a true champion, both on and off the slopes. Her story is far from over, and as she continues to inspire and uplift others, her legacy will live on for generations to come.

04eedc5c-6cef-4aaa-8652-ee8102d41bd0R01